ME AND MY VALENTINE

(AN ANTHOLOGY OF POEMS)
(PAPERBACK, 1ST EDITION, FEB 2023)

COMPILED AND EDITED BY:
DR. SONIA GUPTA

Dedicated to

Every ♥ That

Knows to Love

Contents

Preface ix

Foreword xiii

The Gardens Of Love xix

Poems Inspiring To Celebrate Love xxv

Acknowledgements xxix

Biography Of The Editor xxxi

Me And My Valentine xxxvii

List Of Poets xxxix

1. How Do I ? 1

2. Only For You 3

3. Hide And Seek 5

4. I Am In Love With You 7

5. Valentine's Soft Touch 9

6. To Someone Special 11

7. Never Let Me Go 13

8. Valentine's Day 15

9. A Love Song 17

10. The Happiness Of Love 19

11. Resolute Valentine 21

12. The Sweet Schmaltz Of Spring 23

13. For You 25

14. Loving Tribute To My Beloved 27

15. Meeting Two Beyond 29

16. Waiting For Her 31

17. Feelings 33

18. I Think Only Of You 35

Contents

19. Valentine Day Bash 37

20. My True Valentine 39

21. Divine Kintsugi 41

22. He Owns My Heart 43

23. Eternal Love 45

24. Pleasure Of Majestic Love 47

25. Valentine's Wish 49

26. Withered Flowers 51

27. Valentine's Day Valids Decency 53

28. Once In A Blue Moon 55

29. Lost In Love 57

30. Doorway To My Soul 59

31. Our Grey Destiny 61

32. Honey, The Love Of My Life 63

33. Love Beyond Measures 65

34. My First Valentine 67

35. Dear Love 69

36. My Teddy 71

37. Love Seasons Life 73

38. Rhythm Of Love 75

39. The Labyrinth Of Love 77

40. Deep Feeling 79

41. When Two Souls Combine 81

42. To My Soul 83

43. Blessed Love 85

44. I Will Always Love You 87

Contents

45. My Sweetheart 89

46. I Am A Sunflower 91

47. Melting Moments 93

48. Keep Well 95

49. Expectation 97

50. Is It Not You? 99

Preface

"Love is like the wind, you can't see it but you can feel it."
—Nicholas Sparks

Famous American Novelist 'Nicholas Sparks' has described about LOVE very beautifully that LOVE is like the blowing wind that can't be seen but can be definitely felt within. The word 'LOVE' seems to be very small, but it is like a deep ocean filled with vivid emotions and feelings. LOVE has been a favourite theme of poetry for ages. The sweetness and emotions of LOVE poetry can be well felt while reading and reciting the poems based on Romeo and Juliet, especially in the sonnets composed by the great legend of English literature, 'William Shakespeare'.

LOVE has got some magic wand that creates miracles by leaving a magnificent spell that inspires poets to dip their hidden feelings into the ink of their pen to paint a beautiful canvas that reflects the vivid shades of romance. Romantic poetry is afloat on the high waves of lovable emotions, sometimes ushering like surges of fantasy, sometimes touching upon reality, flowing through the banks of joys and sorrows, passions and pangs, ecstasy and agony, longing and belonging. It originates from deep within the heart expressing unsaid feelings.

'Valentine's Day' which is celebrated on 14th February every year is a day of expressing LOVE to our loved ones. This unique celebration has an ancient history that has been scribbled in the pages of the world's specific occasions. On this day, lovers express their affection toward their beloveds in different ways like through greetings, flowers, sweets and gifts. With the changing vision of the modern world, the significance of this day has also changed at present. Now people have started understanding the actual meaning of the word 'LOVE' which was merely limited to romance. LOVE is not only a romantic feeling but a true bonding between two hearts that is beyond any limitations and without any boundaries. LOVE can be to anyone, to human beings, to any bird, animal or even the lifeless things around. It is not a thing to capture, hold, buy or sell. It is an emotion, a feeling for others whom we love. It is the elixir of life that keeps us alive, a light in the murk, a hope in despair, a smile in pain and food to survive. One single word of LOVE is enough to heal the wounds that persisted for a long, to ignite the willingness to live again, to eradicate all envy and grudges and to perceive the real beauty of this life. The only thing needed is to search for that word and to embrace its existence.

As well said, poetry is the best way to express our hidden feelings and emotions freely. After the successful release of recent anthologies on WOMEN, poets approached me to publish another anthology of poems on the theme 'LOVE' in the joy of celebrating the coming Valentine's Day. That inspired me to take this initiative and the wonderful anthology is in your hands. The current anthology "ME AND MY VALENTINE" is a compilation of 50 poems composed by 50 poets throughout the world. The poets have expressed the vivid colours and shades of 'LOVE' through their verses and painted such a lovable canvas that would be preserved forever in the hearts of readers who after reading these poetic rhymes, will get drowned in the nectar of LOVE. While compiling these poems, one common feeling that my heart felt was that each poem revolved around the LOVE of two lovers, as if a conversation was going on between two hearts, that made an impression in my mind to choose the title as "ME AND MY VALENTINE". After reading these poems, we can perceive the real meaning of the word 'LOVE' and we can find it everywhere around, in humans, in Nature, in relationships, in words, in pains, in smiles and in imagination too.

I will say only one thing here, this is not only a book but a saga of LOVE and its lovers which will be scribbled forever in the history of poetry, reminding us that every day is a Valentine's Day and each moment is to celebrate and cherish the presence of LOVE within and around us. So let us LOVE and spread LOVE everywhere and make this world a lovable place.

Wish you all a magnificent, lovable, joyous and blissful VALENTINE'S DAY.

Dr. Sonia Gupta

Foreword

Dr. Shailesh Gupta Veer (Fatehpur, Uttar Pradesh, India)

Verses Filled with Love and Charm

Love is the most beautiful feeling in this world. Without love, there is nothing. Love is life, and the motion of the world is incomplete without love. Love is the culmination of dedication. Love is the real joy of life. American author Helen Keller said very clearly about love - "The best and most beautiful things in this world cannot be seen or even heard, but must be felt with the heart." Without love, there is nothing. Love is life, and the motion of the world is incomplete without love. Love is the culmination of dedication. Love is the real joy of life. Love is a happy form of union of two beautiful hearts. On the other hand, love is a sad form of separation also. The title makes it clear that the central theme of the anthology "ME AND MY VALENTINE" is 'Love'.

According to great author Khalil Gibran- "Life without love is like a tree without blossoms or fruit." Many poems praising the glory of love enhance the beauty of the anthology. Many times, we take Valentine's Day very superficially, but it is not so. Beliefs of love can be of many colors, and their form can be different, but the essence of all is the same. There is no meaning of materiality without intimacy. The purity of love takes it to its highest form.

What is love? To understand this we need to read the popular English poet of the 17th century, Robert Herrick's poem "Of Love." A concise explanation of the special nature of love can be seen in this poem:-

How Love came in, I do not know,

Whether by th' eye, or ear, or no:

Or whether with the soule it came (At first)

infused with the same:

Whether in part'tis here or there,

Or, like the soule, whole every where:

This troubles me: but as I well

As any other, this can tell;

That when from hence she does depart,

The out-let then is from the heart.

There has been some change in the concepts of love in every era, however, there has been no change in the universal concept of love. Innumerable golden stories of love from many parts of the world are recorded on the pages of history. There are also many vibrant stories of love in Indian tradition and literature, that makes us feel proud. Various colorful and magnificent poems by fifty poets on an important subject like love add to the aura of the anthology and also present a captivating tableau of their love-related concept. The message of these poems is clear, the world is overflowing with the energy of love. This energy of love is the need of the times and society. Love is an important factor in creating a better world and in taking humanity to greater heights.

As an editor, Dr. Sonia Gupta's efforts of presenting an anthology from different poets throughout the world on such a blissful feeling known as 'Love' is highly appreciable. I believe the anthology "ME AND MY VALENTINE" will be widely read and appreciated. And after reading these verses full of love and charm, more love and harmony will flow into our life to make it more blessed and lovable. Hearty congratulations and best wishes to Dr. Sonia Gupta for editing a wonderful compilation and to all the eminent poets involved in it.

Brief Introduction about Dr. Shailesh Gupta Veer

He is a poet, critic, reviewer, editor and multi-prize winner. He is a bilingual, writes in English & Hindi both. He is admin and moderator of various poetry groups on Facebook. He has edited about two dozen literary books and several magazines. His poetry has been published in various literary National and International magazines, journals, anthologies and websites. He has won many awards in the field of literature. His poems have been translated into Chinese, Greek, German, French, Azerbaijani, Arabic, Italian, Serbian, Croatian, Portuguese, Nepali, Punjabi & some other languages. He is the editor of Micro poetry Cosmos and the associate editor of The Voice of Creative Research. He was declared a Literary Icon in December 2018 by TV program 'You and Literature Today' from Nigeria. His poems were read on 'The Dear John Show of Warrington,' England. He is an inspiration for the budding poets. He is PhD in Archaeology and is currently working as a Government Teacher.

CONTACT DETAILS:

- **Address:** 18/17, Radha Nagar, Fatehpur, UP, India - 212601
- **Mobile :** 9839942005
- **Email ID:** editorsgveer@gmail.com
- **Facebook ID:** https://www.facebook.com/shailesh.veer.39
- **Blog:** https://poetryshailesh.blogspot.com

Buoyant Smile

Now you are not you
while I am still I
your promises were false
but my love was true.

Difficult to believe that
you have left me
your preterition has broken me
but the undying longing to live still remains.

Nicely you should understand it-
there is much more beyond you;
Want to sit in the lap of nature for a while,
so that on the face again
I can bring a buoyant smile.

© **Dr. Shailesh Gupta Veer**

The Gardens Of Love

Stoianka Boianova (Sofia, Bulgaria)

There is no greater happiness than loving and being loved. The most important of all basic human psychological needs is love.

The title of the anthology "ME AND MY VALENTINE" invites us to a holiday - as early as the 14th century in England, the tradition of exchanging love messages, called "valentines", began. Modern symbols of love are objects and sweets with the shape of a heart, as well as images of a winged Cupid. The most popular gifts are roses and chocolate in a shiny red heart-shaped package.

The poems in the anthology, which are kind of valentines, are filled with charm, magnetism, sublimity, romance and dreaminess. They flow from one to another and describe a dreamy world filled with love, anticipation, excitement, dances, lips, wings, suns. We live in this world because of the beloved. We are cheerful and playful. We flirt and laugh; we wonder that we have lived to the point of happiness, we can look into each other's eyes, enveloped in the intoxication and gratitude of the moment. When the loved one is far from us, we feel confused, lost, hopeless.

Love is wealth, waiting for it is exciting and painful, we look at the horizon with hope, under the moon, by the sea, everywhere - we will draw it, dream and feel it with the breeze. If we find it - it is immortal and majestic. Love is a tender flower in the fairy garden of life. Roses, the flowers of love, bloom in the intoxicating garden. For Valentine's Day, 50 million roses, 1 billion cards, millions of gifts, hearts, bubbles and kisses are given around the world.

Roses are a symbol of passion and romance. According to legend, they were the favorite flowers of Venus, the Roman goddess of love. Roses - I spent my childhood in the fragrant Valley of the Roses under the peaks of the Balkan Mountains, in the country whose national symbol is Rosa damascena - Bulgaria. We welcome the newborn with roses, marry with roses, and disappear among roses.

In the poems of the anthology, the garden is divine. When we are in love - we reach Heaven. There, two people feel as one - holding hands, they walk together on the common path, in the direction indicated by God. The souls are together, the eyes shine, caught in the magic of the great feeling. They will be together until death. And after that. We were created with God's love that fills us. The need to love and be loved is ingrained in us humans. It is a stepping stone that brings us closer to God's kingdom and greatness. The verses fill us with harmony, we feel loved, uplifted, we fly to exciting worlds and settlements. Anthology of Love Poems shows that we are moving towards the age of love. With a dream - that the laws of love become our essence.

Dr. Sonia Gupta is a well-known name in the literature who has already established herself as an independent author of a total of sixteen books till date and as an editor, she has edited several anthologies, poems, magazines, and write-ups of many poets from the world. Presenting an anthology on such a beautiful theme called 'Love' is one of her other achievements as an editor. The selection of poems by her has led to the compilation of a wonderful anthology that is well-appreciated. I congratulate Dr. Sonia Gupta and all the versatile poets included in the anthology for their tremendous efforts and passion. I am assured, these verses will touch the hearts of readers leaving a magical spell.

Biography of Stoianka Boianova

She is a poet, writer, author, editor and reviewer. She has authored eleven books: poetry, novel and short stories. and co-authored three bilingual books, poetry and haiku – in India with Minko Tanev. She has participated in over 60 international anthologies and publications with numerous awards and recognitions. She edits dictionaries and books. She is in the European Top 100 of the most creative haiku authors. She won several awards, "First World Poetry Competition of Newspapers and Televisions", 2020, China, Chinese International Zhengxin Poet Award, 2022, International Poetry Prize "Ossi di Seppia", 2023, Italy. She is a Chairwoman of Haiku Club – Plovdiv, an editorial board member of "Haiku Sviat/Haiku World" magazine. She is also a member of PEN Bulgaria, Union of the Bulgarian Writers, the Bulgarian haiku Union, the Haiku Foundation – USA, United Haiku and Tanka Society – UK, the World Haiku Association, Japan, Global Honorary Council of Federation of World Culture & Art Society (Singapore). She is a Physicist and has worked in the field of measurement accuracy - metrology, standardization, certification, authorization.

- **Email ID**: stboianova@abv.bg
- **Facebook ID**: https://www.facebook.com/stoianka.boianova.3

Through the Ages

We met when God created the worlds,
and filled them with his love.
Then we got lost because we were scattered
in the edges of the universe.

I have kept the memory of you since that time,
Since then, the sun has been rising thousand times,
the moon has been going down thousand times.

I've been waiting for you thousand days,
thousand nights I've been dreaming of you ...
On how many planets I've searched for you.
How many galaxies I have passed with flame ...

When we met again,
the light erupted.
The world has expanded,
in it were God, you and me.

© Stoianka Boianva

Poems Inspiring To Celebrate Love

Prince Steve Oyebode (Okuku, Osun, Nigeria)

Isn't it just so great when you find one of those books that completely drags you in, makes you fall in love with the characters, grammatical structures and demands that you sit tight to enjoy the reading of the content? One of such collections of selected literary pieces is "Me and My Valentine", edited and compiled by a renowned writer, poetess and author, Dr. Sonia Gupta whose subversive brilliance shines in new unexpected way with this masterpiece. The anthology is written by fifty international poets of note around the world who have benchmarks in poetry. The hype around this anthology has been unquestionable and admittedly, the one that will make you eager to lay your hands on and read with every sense of enthusiasm.

Valentine's Day is a divine occasion of celebrating and expressing love in a vivid number of ways. Some express it with bouquet of roses, some with gifts, some with music, some with sweets. Whatever the way is, feeling is only one; deep love within the heart. While reading these poems, I could feel the emerging emotions and feelings of poets' hearts as a lover which touch the heart of reader pulling him or her toward the sweet aura of love and leaving no more desire within. It is felt as if whole life has been lived in this lovable moment only. In the hustle and bustle of today's life, we all have forgotten to love, I think. But as a human being our heart yearns to love someone and to be loved by someone. As an editor, Dr. Sonia Gupta has made justification to the title of the collection through her literary dexterity of analysis and explanation on the need to promote and celebrate love in a world of turmoil.

I have found the anthology to be well thought out and the one permeated with love, romance, fulfillment of expectations and maintenance of relationship. I believe, it is a must-read anthology for all the lovers of poetry around the globe. And after reading these poems, everyone will fall in the love with the whole world as Valentine and will cherish the existence of this beautiful blessing gifted by Almighty which is known as 'Love'. I congratulate Dr. Sonia Gupta and all the versatile poets included in this anthology for their tremendous contribution.

Biography of Prince Steve Oyebode

He is a multi-award-winning writer and poet. He is a Founder/President of an international literary forum called "Haven for the world writers" (a forum of Global writers and poets). He is an active member and Admin of various literary groups on Facebook. He keeps on sharing his literary work on several literary platforms. His write-ups are part of many National and International journals, magazines, anthologies and blogs. He has received several recognitions for his literary contribution. He reviews vivid anthologies, poems and write-ups of poets from different regions of the world. He is honored annually by the Indian Government on the auspicious occasion of their Independence Day. He is a graduate of Microbiology (BSc Hons) from the prestigious Obafemi Awolowo University, Ile Ife, Osun state and also bagged a master of science (MSc) in Legal, Criminology & Security Psychology from the University of Ibadan, Oyo state, Nigeria. He is enjoying his professional and literary journey with a great endeavor.

- **Facebook ID:** https://www.facebook.com/oyebode.s.olalekan
- **Email ID:** princestelek@gmail.com

Without Valentine's Day

Just imagine a year without Valentine's Day

Can't just figure it out

Where go all the roses?

What happened to the gifts and cards?

And how better will I search for my soul?

Who deserves my sincere regards.

Surely, I must reach out

To the brain behind my smile

No matter how close or far

I must tell her one more time

How fast my heart longs after

As a Hart pants after water brooks.

Here comes the hour of love

The Valentine's Day is here again

So, I am sending a poem to say

You are so special and rare

A cynosure of my eyes

Happy Valentine my sweetheart.

© Prince Steve Oyebode

Acknowledgements

Gratitude is not merely a word, but deep meaning it beholds. I usually hear these words – "If we say Thank you to someone, it means we are bowing our head in front of that Lord only". We can forget anything in life, but we should never forget to thank someone who has helped or motivated us in any way.

I am a medical professional, I never thought that one day I would become a writer, poet and author. It is all a miracle and a dream for me. But now it has become my passion, inspiration, and an integral part of my life. It's all by God's grace that he honoured me with such a unique gift.

First of all, I thank the Goddess of knowledge and wisdom *Maa Saraswati,*who gave me the strength to complete this work and encouraged me to pick up my pen to compile, edit, and prepare this anthology.

In the world, everything changes, but one thing that never ever changes is *our parents.* Heartfelt thanks to my parents for their faith and showering their infinite blessings on me. Special thanks to my father who has left this materialistic world attaining the embrace of the divine Lord. He had been my inspiration and will be forever and his teachings illuminate my life's pathway like an enlightening candle. Thankyou mom for being there throughout my work and for all your support and blessings.

Huge bundle of thanks to all the authors and poets, who have put their endless efforts by contributing their wonderful poems signifying the theme of this anthology. Most of the poets are much senior to me and I pay my regard and honour to all of them for their full cooperation from the day one of this project till the last moment, respecting my guidelines and instructions. Without all of you, this collection would not have been possible. Once again, my heartfelt thanks to all of you for your love, cooperation and encouragement.

A token of thanks to '*Dr. Shailesh Gupta Veer*' *sir* for writing a wonderful foreword for this anthology and guiding at every step. Thank you sir for all your blessings and support.

My gratitude to the International poets 'Stoianka Boianova'from Bulgaria & 'Prince Steve Oyebod**e**' from Nigeria or taking out their valuable time in writing the reviews about this anthology despite their busy schedules. Thankyou both of you, your words have beautified our anthology.

Teachers are the selfless builders of our life, A word of thanks to all my respected teachers who always showed me the right path in my life and brimmed my heart with their blessings. Lovable token of gratitude to my *brothers, sisters, and all family*members for their love and support always. *Friends* are the precious ornaments gifted by God, who without any blood relation, make a bonding of forever relation. My regards and love to all friends far and near. Last but not least, it will be unfair if I forget to thank the *Notion Press publication* through which this book is going to be published. Thanks to entire team for the cooperation. Thank you, readers, fellow poets and friends for all your love and appreciation.

Dr. Sonia Gupta

Biography Of The Editor

Dr. Sonia Gupta (Mohali, Punjab, India)

Dr. Sonia Gupta is a writer, poet, reviewer, editor and translator. She writes in English, Hindi, and Punjabi languages. By profession, she is a Dentist (MDS) with major specialization in Oral and Maxillofacial Pathology. Poetry is her passion. She writes in vivid genera of literature like poetry, stories, essays, letters, songs and many more. She has established herself as a renowned author after getting her Sixteen independent books published till date, out of which Ten are in English and Six are in Hindi language. Her English books are poetic collections entitled 'Spectrum of Life', 'Canvas of Life..With My Pen', 'Fountain of Inspirations', 'Meeting

My Soulmate', 'Silent Verses', 'Mysterious Musings of Life', 'Agony of Life', 'Miracle of Virtues', 'Acrostic Motivations', and 'There is No Darkness'. Her first English novel is coming soon. Her Hindi books include Five collections of poetry entitled 'Zindagi Gulzar Hai', 'Ummid Ka Diya', 'Kabhi Jalte Kabhi Bujhte Chirag', 'Kuch Ankahe Ehsas' and 'Prkriti Ki Gungunahat' and one collection of stories entitled 'Aadmi Bne Rehne Ka Dhong'.

Her literary journey continues with a great endeavour. She has gone through many ups and downs in her life that directed her vision toward suffering and she expresses that with her pen. Her writings reflect her closeness and deep love for nature, life, spirituality and humanity. For her, poetry is a God-gifted boon and she wishes to fly high wearing the wings of poetry. She has contributed to more than 100 National and International English anthologies so far. She is a regular contributor to various National and International magazines, newspapers and journals. She has translated many poems by other poets from different regions of the world into English, Hindi and Punjabi languages. She runs a blog about the Punjabi translation of English poems by different poets throughout the world. Her first poetry book in the Punjabi language is coming soon. She is an active member of various poetry groups on Facebook and has won several awards in writing competitions organized by these groups and other literary platforms. She won a Gold and Silver Medal in a Poetic world Cup contest held by Nigeria in Feb and May 2018 respectively, PRASANNA JENN MEMORIAL AWARD -2018 by the Asian Literary Society, and 5th rank in the International Essay writing competition on 'Skin complexion discrimination' organized by literary society, India in March 2018. One of her essays 'Our role & responsibilities toward nation was selected in a National essay writing competition and is a part of the book 'Youth as Nation Builders; a collection of 41 essays published by Lab Academia.

She is a famous name in Hindi literature also. She writes stories, essays, letters, articles, and vivid genera of Hindi poetry. Besides her independent Hindi books, her Hindi writings are part of several International and National anthologies, newspapers, journals and magazines. She has won many awards for her Hindi writings. Her many projects are underway.

Besides poetry, she is fond of painting, singing, cooking, teaching, reading, knitting, designing, stitching and embroidery. She has won many awards in Art competitions. Many of her paintings have been placed on the cover pages of various anthologies. Even she herself designed the cover pages of her two English anthologies entitled "Fountain of Inspirations" and "Canvas of Life...With My Pen". She is actively contributing to the literature via her literary YouTube channel, Facebook page, Blog and Instagram page.

Born and brought up in the family of well-educated people, Dr. Sonia is living her life with simplicity and a mission of doing something meaningful. She considers her family her biggest inspiration, who has always motivated her in each and every phase of her life. She feels proud to have such Grandparents who have enriched their children and grandchildren with ideal virtues and morals. Her grandfather is retired from the Indian Army and serves selflessly for society till today even being reached at the age of 97 Years and believes in doing his tasks on his own. Her grandmother left this materialistic world in 2020. She was a homemaker, who not only taught her Hindi language since her birth but also made her capable of learning other skills like cooking, knitting and embroidery. Dr. Sonia lost her father Late Sh. Devinder Kumar in 2019, who was retired as an English Lecturer from Govt. Senior Secondary School near their hometown. He lived his entire life for his children's bright future and it is his efforts that have let Dr. Sonia and her brothers achieve their goals. As a teacher, he was a renowned name in academics who guided a number of students who are working in well-recognized positions in society today. She is living her life following his teachings and footprints. Her mother, Mrs. Nirmal Devi is retired as a Private Secretary from the Higher Education Dept. Panchkula, Haryana. She is her best friend who has always motivated and accompanied her in her every adventure, whether related to her profession, passion or personal life. She has got two younger brothers, and she considers them the pillars of her life. She feels fortunate to find such brothers who have always stood beside her in even the darkest phases of her life, encouraging her to move ahead. One of her brothers works as a project manager at USA based company in Houston, Texas, USA. And youngest one is acting as a manager in MARUTI company, Manesar, Gurugram, Haryana. He is a professional singer also and is training his 8 - years old son in classical music. She feels blissful to get many teachers who not only taught her professional skills but also appreciated her passionate ventures and today also clap for her achievements. As a person, she is less talkative, simple, humble, hard-working and determined personality. She prefers to utilize every single moment in doing something meaningful rather than wasting in gossiping. She loves to work in a disciplined and organized way. She has completed her many poetry books while traveling to her work place. She is a deep believer in God and a great devotee of Lord Krishna. She is a member of the 'Mahila Mandal Sangeet Samiti' of many temples in her region and frequently participates in various religious events where she sings religious songs composed with her own pen. Her many religious books are in the process of publication.

Dr. Sonia Gupta is a renowned name in her professional field also. She is working as an Associate Professor in the Oral Pathology Dept. at a Dental College in Mohali. She is also pursuing a fellowship program in Forensic

Odontology by the Indian Board of Forensic Odontology. She serves the community as a doctor by providing dental care. She has got several scientific publications in PubMed and Scopus-indexed National and International Journals with the first authorship and many more are under review. She is also working on three textbooks on her subject of specialization. She is acting as a reviewer of various Medical and Dental Journals. She actively takes part in various conferences, workshops, community health programs, and events and has presented several research papers and posters. She is a dedicated academician with a goal of making her students excel in their subjects and in developing their multitalented skills. She is enjoying her professional as well as literary journey full of passion and mission.

CONTACT DETAILS:

- **ADDRESS**- #95/3, Adarsh Nagar, Dera Bassi, Dist: Mohali, Punjab-140507, India.
- **MOBILE**- 6280420736
- **FACEBOOK ID** - 100004964983747@facebook.com
- **FACEBOOK PAGE** - https://www.facebook.com/sonia4840/
- **BLOG** - http://drsoniablogspot.blogspot.in/
- **PUNJABI TRANSLATION BLOG** - http://passionatepunjabijourney.blogspot.com/
- **E MAIL** -drsoniagupta82@gmail.com
- **YOUTUBE CHANNEL**https://www.youtube.com/channel/UCKF2jM5P8VDjZ9fBZLBTRHA
- **INSTAGRAM ID**-https://instagram.com/gdrsonia?igshid=YmMyMTA2M2Y=

Me And My Valentine

We found our love beyond the eight rivers,
There our lust and laughter floated in waves,
Our voices glistened like broken silvers,
We made our oaths to the Gods in their caves.

To earth, heavens have proclaimed you my spouse,
I long to live always in your embrace,
And kiss your soft lips till the Starlight rouse,
Your aura, I breathe, a blessings of grace.

O, I will kiss the floor before your feet,
I will honour your failings till time stops,
I will pull the sun down when the clouds sleet,
And make love to you on the mountain top.

You're my miss world... My miss valentine.
My love for you is from the heart of vine.

© Dr. Sonia Gupta

List Of Poets

S. No.	POET'S NAME	PAGE No.
1.	Aarti Mittal	1-2
2.	Aditi Karthick	3-4
3.	Ajayi Oluwasegun Samson	5-6
4.	Alok Mishra	7-8
5.	Anil Gupta	9-10
6.	Anju Charanjith	11-12
7.	Dr. Balesh Jindal	13-14
8.	Basudev Paul	15-16
9.	Bharati Nayak	17-18
10.	Binod Dawadi	19-20
11.	Bipul Chandra Kalita	21-22
12.	Birendu Kumar Sinha	23-24
13.	Boby Borah	25-26
14.	B. S. Saroja	27-28
15.	Damodar Boruah	29-30
16.	Dashrath Naik	31-32
17.	Dr. Gangalaxmi Patnaik	33-34
18.	Gargi Saha	35-36
19.	Dr. Hitendra Mehta	37-38
20.	Kamar Sultana Sheik	39-40
21.	Lakshmi Ajoy	41-42
22.	Madelyn Fernandez-Marcelino	43-44
23.	Madhuri Kulkarni	45-46
24.	Maid Corbic	47-48
25.	Manaswinee Dash Panigrahi	49-50

S. NO.	POET'S NAME	PAGE NO.
26.	Pradnya Surve	51-52
27.	Prasanna Bhatta	53-54
28.	Prasanna Kumar Mohapatra	55-56
29.	Promila Punnu Bhardwaj	57-58
30.	Rachana Sood	59-60
31.	Rajendra K Padhi	61-62
32.	Rajesh Sharma Brahmabhatla	63-64
33.	Ranjana Kashyap	65-66
34.	Ravi thakur	67-68
35.	Rimni Chakravarty	69-70
36.	Rohit Dash	71-72
37.	Sane Shiva Shankar	73-74
38.	Seema Sharma	75-76
39.	Shafia Afzal	77-78
40.	Shelleyandra Kapil	79-80
41.	Shwetha A	81-82
42.	Sreedharan Parokode	83-84
43.	Srividya Subramanian	85-86
44.	Dr. Suboohi Jafar	87-88
45.	Sudipta Mishra	89-90
46.	Sulekha Samantaray	91-92
47.	Sulochana Narayanan	93-94
48.	Sumi Kapahera	95-96
49.	Swapan Kumar Rakshit	97-98
50.	Unnikrishnan Atiyodi	99-100

AN ANTHOLOGY OF POEMS
(PAPERBACK, 1ST EDITION, FEBRUARY 2023)
COMPILED & EDITED BY
DR. SONIA GUPTA

1. How Do I ?

How do I look at you?
Your eyes behind your tinted glasses gaze at me,
I wonder, what do they read,
From head to toe,
My pulchritude feels shy,
My soft juicy lips wish to taste you,
My eyes wish to dive deep into you.

I wish to be in your arms,
Feel your embrace,
Feel your touch hide in you
But how do I ?
Your notorious eyes,
Catch hold of me,
And my eyes….
Smile and shy.

© Aarti Mittal

Aarti Mittal (Mumbai, Maharashtra, India)

aarti.amittal@gmail.com

She is a bilingual poet who writes in English & Hindi languages. She writes short skits with morals for children. She follows the religion of humanity, compassion and love and tries to spread the same. She believes that her writings can win hearts and help to bring some change to make this world a better place. Her writings also include themes based on women's empowerment and child exploitation. She is B.A. B.Ed and pursuing M.A. Currently, she is working as a teacher.

2. Only For You

I am red,
You are blue.
Fire and water,
The poles of a magnet too.

Souls intertwined,
My mind on your tow.
I fall into your cradle of comfort,
A safe place to go.

You are the one who extinguishes my worries,
My only faith and pride.
The hand I can hold on to,
And my sole guide.

Never letting go,
Never tracing apart.
My true enlightenment,
Lies within your heart.

© Aditi Karthick

Aditi Karthick (Chennai, Tamil Nādu, India)

vmpselvi@gmail.com

She is a 13-year-old young writer who wrote her first poem 'I love you Mom' when she was in Kindergarten and won first prize at the Minnesota State Fair. She loves reading and writing poems and stories. She is also fond of creating digital illustrations. She wishes to fly high wearing the wings of poetry.

3. Hide and Seek

I want a world where we will play hide and seek,
Without you finding a secret place to hide,
From an open space, I can throw you a peek,
My heart is the only hidden place you can bide,
Looking and laughing at you from afar,
See you smiling like the brightening of a star,
Gazing at your shining face leaves my mouth ajar.

I know a land, so lawless and flawless,
Where crime is committed without any punishment,
The calming voice of the sea arouses full alertness,
Our sleeping eyes from slumber, awakening into a great astonishment,
A fertile land growing precious fruit for our nourishment.
If I tell you of a beautiful lawless land of love,
Would you follow me there to play hide and seek ?

What better time to play this childish game ?
You hide... I seek, we both get lost, who do we blame?

© Ajayi Oluwasegun Samson

Ajayi Oluwasegun Samson (Osogtbo, Osun, Nigeria)

ajayiolusegun49@gmail.com

He is a poet and a creative writer. Poetry is his passion. He writes poems, essays and stories since secondary school. He has won several prizes and awards during his schooling both at the National and Local levels, in debate competitions and essay writing. He is an active member of several poetry groups on Facebook. Presently, he is pursuing Nursing.

4. I Am in Love With You

When my conscience gets restless,
My silent breaths cry,
My impatient eyes lose their sight,
I come to know…
I am in love with you.

When rays of the budding sun,
Pierce my innocent feelings,
When a moment to me seems a tears-laden year,
I come to know…
I am in love with you.

When lost is the self-mine,
In the colour of the blue ocean of your eyes,
I feel my journey is complete,
I come to know…
I am in love with you.

© Alok Mishra

Alok Mishra (Sitapur, Uttar Pradesh, India)

alokk2129@gmail.com

He is an award-winning bilingual (English & Hindi) poet, critic, reviewer and editor. He is Admin of a poetry group "Literature Lover Association" on Facebook. His poems are published in several National and International anthologies, newspapers and magazines. He has edited 6 anthologies of English poems. He is M. Phil in English and presently working as a Government teacher. He is also an astrologer.

5. Valentine's Soft Touch

On Valentine's Day…
I went to the park
With a bouquet to propose to my fiancée.
My heart was full of happiness…
But a thought in my mind was also arising
That he might get angry.

At the same time…
I felt a soft touch on my shoulder,
I turned around…and saw…
The thread of life standing in front of me.
Those lovable words my ears listened to…

'I love you', I love you very much,
I will fill your life with happiness,
I accept your offer,
My face started smiling …
The twinkling stars in the sky were looking at us.
Becoming the witness of our everlasting bond of love.

© Anil Gupta

Anil Gupta (Ujjain, Madhya Pradesh, India)

guptamedicose14@gmail.com

He is a bilingual poet and writer who writes in English and Hindi languages. He has authored a book entitled "History of Ujjayini and greatness of Simhastha". He is an active member of various poetry groups on Facebook and participates in many poetry contests. His writings are part of several National and International magazines, newspapers and anthologies. He has won several awards for her poetry. He is an editor of the newspaper 'Mahakal Brahman. He is also a Senior Correspondent of Doordarshan Bhopal Canter —Ujjain. He is MSc, LLB, and M.J.M.C. Currently, he is working as a Pharmacist and Journalist.

6. To Someone Special

I have nothing to give but only my love,
My unstinting and candid love, the message of God.
The comfort of broken hearts,
And the breath of loving ones.

The divine theory of nature that keeps eternity,
You lifted my soul to the ultimate ecstasy.
You gave me serenity for my spiritual growth,
You made me a complete woman.

With your sweet loving touch and care,
You changed my world of existence.
You are the string of my life,
You are the voice of my heart.

You are the music of my soul,
You are my strength and desire.
You are my entire worth and nobility,
You are my valentine, O' buddy.

© Anju Charanjith

Anju Charanjith (Muscat, Oman)

anjucharanjith@gmail.com

She is a poet and writer. She is an active member of various poetry groups on Facebook and participates in many poetry contests. Her writings are part of several National and International magazines, newspapers and anthologies. She has won several awards for her poetry. She is a TESOL graduate and is pursuing the International PG Diploma in TESOL/ TEFL program. Presently she works in the Sultanate of Oman.

7. Never Let Me Go

When the raindrops flow,
Into the dirty furrows.
When the brazen breeze,
Plunges me into the deepest despair,
When my wretched smile,
Woefully, becomes a tear.

When memories of togetherness,
Start to fade away,
When my heart becomes,
Forsaken in forlornness,
Then my dear, never let me go.
NEVER LET ME GO.

© Dr. Balesh Jindal

Dr. Balesh Jindal (Delhi, India)

jindalbalesh@yahoo.co.in

She is a renowned artist with a creative portfolio of art, poetry and photographs. She has published three poetry books; a coffee table book 'A Hundred Dreams', 'Dear Father' and 'The Reluctant Doctor a Memoir'. She is a physician by profession; a graduate of the prestigious Lady Hardinge Medical College in Delhi and has had a professional medical practice for the last forty years. She has received several awards in her professional and literary fields.

8. Valentine's Day

This is a celebration of love and affection
It could be termed a feasting day
It could mean a lot of love as loader, fete
It could retain a sustained strain of flame.

The person one can never let go beyond
This carries something bigger
Something beyond the reach of the human bond
An undertow always pulls you back in.

No one knows but an urge, a dictate throbs
Like crushes make you feel crazy pulses
Bashfulness resides in your giddy feeling
So, the two terms are like a huge oak.

These have caught up the universal spectra
Varied in feeling, diverse in manifestation
This is held soft in great affection by people
Wallowing in love rainbow, in magnificence.

© Basudev Paul

Basudev Paul (Malbazar, West Bengal, India)

basudevpaul01@gmail.com

He is a poet, writer and author. His poetry is a psalm; a sacred song of his life felt at the gloaming of his career. His poetical composition aiming at the worship of God chants as a canticle for humanity. He has published one English poetry book; "The Permanent Transient". He is M.A. in English and has worked as a teacher with thirty-seven years of teaching experience.

9. A Love Song

Dear, I love you, but YOU are not you.
YOU are that beauty that fills me with light.
YOU are that hand that picks out the thorns from my feet.
YOU are that presence that is ever present in my happiness and darkness,

In my cloudy sky, YOU are the color that makes the rainbow.
YOU appear as the North star in directionless weather.
YOU are not the Rose but the red of the Rose,
And the thorns that Guard the Rose,
YOU are the song of the songbird.
Blue of the Blue-sky, and Green of the Green-leaves.

It doesn't matter where YOU live.
For I feel YOU as the oxygen-filled air circulating around me.
And YOU will stay here...
As a shaft of light,
And the last piece of my breath.

© Bharati Nayak

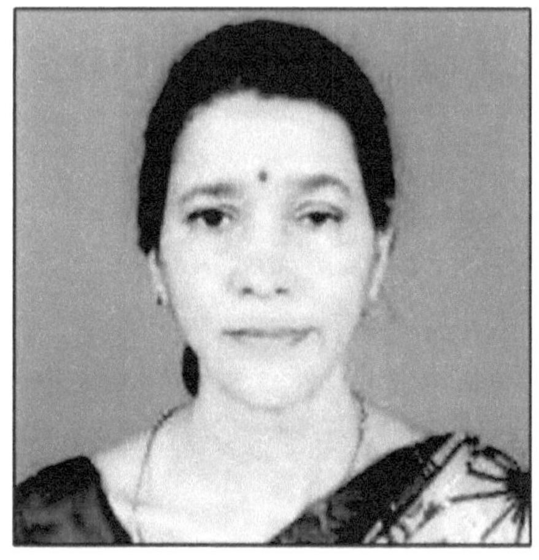

Bharati Nayak (Bhubaneswar, Odisha, India)

bharati1962@rediffmail.com

She is a bilingual (English & Odia) poet, writer, translator and editor. She has so far published two Odia poetry collections, one book of translation of South African poetess Adiela Akkoo's book 'Lost in A Quatrain' into Odia, two English poetry collections as sole author and six books as co-author with other poets. She is a postgraduate in Political Science. She is retired as Under Secretary from the Revenue & Disaster Management Department, Odisha.

10. The Happiness of Love

Why do people love?

How do they get happiness, in the love?

I don't know,

I have not fallen in the love,

I am so innocent and kind.

If you are there O' my lover,

In any part of the world,

Come into my life,

And.. teach me how to do love?

How to get happiness from love?

I am waiting for you, my dear,

I hope one day you will come back,

In my life,

To make me feel, what is love?

And…to make my world full of love.

© Binod Dawadi

Binod Dawadi (Napal, Kathmandu)

vinoddawadi9@gmail.com

He is a poet, writer and author. He has authored one book; 'The Power of Words'. He has worked on more than 1000 anthologies and renowned magazines. His vision is to change society through knowledge, so he wants to provide enlightenment to people through his writing skills. He is a master's degree holder in Major English and is currently working in a private consultancy company.

11. Resolute Valentine

My resolute valentine eyes me not in public,
Soft she may be inside,
But being dropped out unexpectedly,
Her anger rises to the height of inflexibility.

I ignored her once upon a valentine's day
To purify my love,
Cranky feelings cranked us,
To make things fall against our maturity.

On this tempting day of love, I stand still,
Eying my road broadly,
Letting my searching sight catch your presence,
And, scrutinizing the ego that made the difference.

Valentine's whistles bring me back from sadness,
I buy roses or plant the thorny tree,
To keep my love for my dearest love alive,
Keeping aside the divine gift's profit and loss account.

© Bipul Chandra Kalita

Bipul Chandra Kalita (Nagaon, Assam, India)

bipulkalita074@gmail.com

He is a trilingual poet who writes in Assamese, Hindi and English language. He has authored three books. He has edited many journals and literary anthologies. His writings have been published in many National and International magazines, newspapers and anthologies. He has authored nearly 26 Assamese plays. He is M.A. in English and currently working as a post-graduate teacher.

12. The Sweet Schmaltz of Spring

Hear the footfall of the Spring queen,
Bride like looking in the floral palanquin,
From icy aloofness to bustling weather,
The season arrives with bounteous treasure.

Ripples of joy and spray of lovable colours,
Festivity bursting beyond any measure.
Tracking plains, ocean and space,
Migratory birds seen landing in grace.

Thirsty throats of love hearts parching,
With amorous cravings moonlight marching,
The lush green abundance of the silver mat,
Embracing lip-locking from ambrosial vat.

O' look, in the lap of spring, love blooms like flowers,
Lovers dance and enjoy embracing together,
Spring is a season of valentine's merriment,
The sweet schmaltz of nature's embellishment.

© Birendu Kumar Sinha

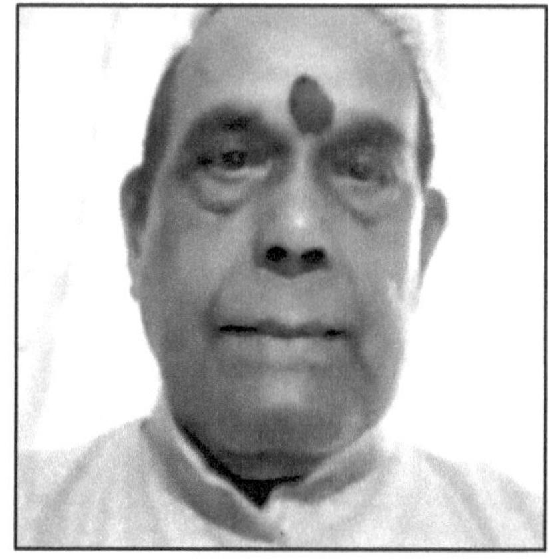

Birendu Kumar Sinha (Patna, Bihar, India)

birenduksinha14@gmail.com

He is a freelance journalist, short story writer and poet. He has authored two poetry books namely 'Fragrance of earth' and 'Symphony of love'. He is an active member of various poetic forms on Facebook. He has won several awards for his poems. He served as a English lecturer and Senior Management Officer at State Bank of India.

13. For You

I can wait for you…
Secretly behind shadows,
A fresh wind may tell me in a whisper,
The message of your arrival.
The blue sky may watch with envious eyes,
An intimate silhouette will reflect, in the smiles of green.
I may recite a poem in noon too for you,
Putting eye to eye on you.

I can tell a tale of the witching hour,
In the deep and dense darkness of night,
Two fireflies are on a boat embracing the vast sea,
I'll wait being a handful of dust,
Mixing with crazy wind,
I'll wait for you…
Secretly behind the lotus petals,
Being anxious sunshine.

© Boby Borah

Boby Borah (Tinsukia, Assam, India)

bobyborah30@gmail.com

She is a poet and author. She has authored three books and edited several magazines. Her poems and articles are published in several newspapers in Assam. She has been awarded several awards in her professional and literary journey. She is M.A. in literature, Founder / Principal of Shankardev Shishu Niketan school. She is also the president of Doom Dooma Mahila Samiti and secretary of Sundoram Kobi Sanmilan.

14. Loving Tribute to My Beloved

This rose is just a symbol,
Expressing my love through acts,
I nourish it till times eternal,
It's my daily Valentine's gift for you,
On this sacred day, you awakened my love.

The beauty of thy soul,
Took me into the garden,
Full of sublime flowers,
Spreading the fragrance of love,
To the core of my being.

Oh, the poetry of my life,
You transformed my solitude into mirthful moments,
Filled the silence of nights with soulful notes of love.
On this day of valentine, I gift my pristine loving bond,
Wishing its radiance to stay forever.

© B.S.Saroja

B. S. Saroja (Bangalore, Karnataka, India)

bssaroja1953@gmail.com

She is a poet, writer and author. Her poems and writes have been published in many anthologies, magazines, and periodicals. Poetry is her lifelong passion. She is also a social worker. She is a postgraduate in Kannada and a graduate in Science and a Diploma holder in Commerce and is retired as a personal secretary to the Managing Director of a business organization.

15. Meeting Two Beyond

In search of love, I met you all of a sudden,
Never thought she would be you,
Today you have become my shadow,
Whenever I go, you go beside,
When you go, I go beside,
A meeting will go much beyond a just relation.

Spring without the cuckoo, is it called spring ?
Ahinsa without Gandhi, can it be possible ?
Assam without the Brahmaputra, how can it be possible?
Without you, how my life's battle can be conquerable?

Speaking thoughtfully like wintry rainfall,
When plants struggle for a bath,
For the whole body covered with pollutants,
In my darkest moment, when I become helpless,
Your voice, and little smile enliven me to dance on and on.

© Damodar Boruah

Damodar Boruah (Dergaon, Assam, India)

damodarboruah14@gmail.com

He is a multi-award-winning poet, writer and translator at the National and International levels. He has composed more than five hundred poems to date. He is an active member of various poetry groups on social media. His recent book 'From A Father to A Daughter…to touch the sky!' has become a great hit. His motto: 'Create Farmers, Create Entrepreneurs, Create Markets, Create Stories.' is widely accepted among many stakeholders. He holds a degree of B.Sc(Hons), GNIIT and DBM. By profession, he is a small tea grower and farmer.

16. Waiting For Her

With radiant hues,
She drops in triumphant,
With glow galore.

Her thrills and kisses,
Mesmerizing bliss,
Smile she does harbour.

Here I wait patiently,
For her warm hug,
Flavoured with breeze.

She, next to my heart..
A crazy lover of me,
For her spell I beseech.

© Dasharath Naik

Dasharath Naik (Sundargarh, Odisha, India)

dasharath23664@gmail.com

He is a poet, writer and an editor. Poetry is his passion and he writes for pleasure. His main motto is to spread peace, love, and humanity through his poetry. He is the Admin of various poetry groups on Facebook. He has contributed to several anthologies, magazines, and journals, both Nationally and Internationally. He is M.A.,M.Phil. in English. Currently, he is working as a Reader (SS) in English.

17. Feelings

You didn't tell how much love needed to quench thirst,
I would have given love surely a sea of it.

You only needed my blood's still,
Silent twinkling, light breath,
and I flooded my love with my lovely winter warmth.

My love has worn wings, fled away you me abandoning,
keeping me awake watching , waiting,
to the bright twilight evening.

This love act impels to dreams, for dreams fructify love,
my loving you, feelings with such sureness are always genuine.

I choose to be special , wooing never ends, it's reciprocal ,
amid throat cutting,
desires without end our love a parallel.

These dreams alone,
sweeten my feelings, I would have chosen,
I cannot live without you perhaps I pass away, fallen.

© Dr. Gangalaxmi Patnaik

Dr. Gangalaxmi Patnaik (Bangalore, Karnataka, India)

gangalaxmi80@gmail.com

She is a bilingual poet who writes in English and Odia languages. She is an active member of various literary groups on Facebook. She writes in vivid genera of poetry. Her writings are part of several National and International magazines, newspapers and anthologies. She actively participates in various poetry recitation fests. She has won several awards in English literature. She is M.A and PhD in English and a former Associate Professor in English.

18. I Think Only of You

I think only of you,
You are the diamond among the few,
You are my contemplation,
My concentration and meditation.

The love you gave me,
From the superstitions you freed me,
I am in agony,
In anguish.

In melancholy,
Complete disharmony,
In dissatisfaction,
And frustration.
Lovers are like melons,
Shall I tell you why?
To find one good one,
You shall a hundred try.

© Gargi Saha

Gargi Saha (Varanasi, Uttar Pradesh, India)

gargi.paik@gmail.com

She is a creative writer since her childhood. She has published two poetry books namely 'The Muse in My Salad Days' and 'Letters to Him'. Recently she received the Rabindranath Tagore Memorial Award and the Independence day award for poetry. She is a member of various poetry groups on Facebook. She is M.A and M.Phil. in English. Presently she edits several scientific research papers.

19. Valentine Day Bash

At Valentine Day bash, I reached
along with my Love, Mom and Guru

All others were in lovey-dovey pairs
Seeing our foursome, a lover made a jibe
"Boy, this is Valentine's Day meet
You seem to be on an outing with family"

I smilingly replied
"Valentine is about love and strength
All with me are epitome of love in my life
All infuse srength, all are my Valentines"

Unlocking his palm from his lover's palm
With eyes down, lover patted me saying,
"Yours is a true Valentine's Day celebration
upholding the pristine spirit of Valentine"

© Dr. Hitendra Mehta

Dr. Hitendra Mehta (Mumbai, Maharashtra, India)

hitendramehta@rediffmail.com

He is an IIM L Alumnus and a Polymath- poet, artist, social activist and socio-economic thinker, He was a semi-finalist in International Poetry Contest, and Silver Medallist in the All India Drawing Competition. He has authored two books. He is a member of the World Human Rights Protection, Commission, a volunteer at the UN Online Volunteer Program, and featured in Gujarati Midday and Tata Sky interview. He is retired as CEO from Aifso Technologies.

20. My True Valentine

Red Rose,

At Lotus Feet...

No poetry, no prose

Just my heartbeat;

No litany, no song..

Just my life-breath.

No bell nor gong

Just my blood

Gushing in my veins;

Neither incense

Nor lighted lamp

Just in my palms-bowl.

The fragrance and light of my soul.

No fruit nor sweet is in offering

Just my Being, whole...

I place in Thine,

My Guru, my true Valentine.

© Kamar Sultana Sheik

Kamar Sultana Sheik (Bangalore, Karnataka, India)

sultana_sheik@yahoo.co.in

She is a poet, writing mostly on themes of spirituality, mysticism and nature with a focus on Sufi Poetry. She has contributed to various anthologies and won several prizes. Her most recent publication,' The Golden Dawn' (A Covid Times release) won the Poet of the year award 2020 from Galaxy Foundation. She creates artwork to create environmental awareness. A blogger and content writer, Sultana calls herself a wordsmith. She is a post-graduate in Botany and worked in her professional career spanning 18 years.

21. Divine Kintsugi

To the most significant aura surrounding my life,
The most beautiful experience of my soul, surreal magnet of my heart,
Yet another year of being blessed with the divinity of your presence,
For it brought you to this planet, to complete the meaning,
And truest purpose towards my ultimate goal.

Without the Divine experience of your lessons,
I could have never been able, to fill in the vacuumed crevices,
That can only be sealed with your presence and love.

You are my 'Kintsugi',
The Japanese art of putting broken pottery pieces back together with gold,
You are my metaphor for helping me embrace,
All my flaws and imperfections towards beauty and perfection.

You are that gold who fills my broken cracks,
To help me achieve that perfect balance toward completion,
I shall only remain incomplete without You,
For you alone are my Divine Love.

© Lakshmi Ajoy

Lakshmi Ajoy (Mumbai, Maharashtra, India)

ashwini04182@gmail.com

She is a writer, artist, photographer, solo traveller, adventure sports enthusiast, mountaineer and social worker. She is a member of various poetry groups on Facebook and has won several awards. Her aim is to spread happiness and joy all around and help others realize the value and essence of life. Writing helps her to give wings to her imagination and live her dreams. Currently, she works as a spiritual healer and entrepreneur.

22. He Owns My Heart

Somewhere in the universe, some winged knight loves me,
He owns my heart, he found in the abyss,
Down the dark, deep ocean, exalted among pearls,
Born through the years from bitter-salt tears of mother oysters.

He plucked me from the fabled giant clam,
Cozy and warm, the feel of his palm,
My world newly created,
Mystical, as the light years reach of the stars,
My pulsebeats quiver with his arrow-sword when he moves.

Somewhere in the universe, my heart is…
Where my God-knight- rescuer,
Enamoured of my soul, plucks the strings,
I sing with him in the morning,
Till I fall asleep at eventide,
Somewhere in the universe...
This cupid-knight—he owns my heart.

© **Madelyn Fernandez-Marcelino**

Madelyn Fernandez-Marcelino

(Barotac Viejo, Iloilo, Philippines)

christyballadares@gmail.com

She is a writer, poet and author. She is a passionate lover of nature. She is an active member of various literary groups on Facebook and has won several awards in poetry. Her poems are placed in several National and International newspapers, anthologies and magazines. She holds a B.A. degree.She is a teacher and speech coach.

23. Eternal Love

Neither the drizzle nor the downpour,
Stopped them from meeting each other,
The park, the people, the noise around,
Didn't seem to matter.

The bare tree stood witness to the love,
Streaming from their hearts,
As they stood together. Hands clasped,
She looked up into his eyes adoringly.

His reciprocating smile,
Gentle and warm,
The breeze passed by lovingly,
Her body quivered in delight.

A blissful moment it is,
When the two hearts unite,
Vowing to be together,
Lovers forever.

© Madhuri Kulkarni

Madhuri Kulkarni (Bangalore, Karnatka, India)

gouriraj69@gmail.com

She is a bilingual poet who writes in English and Kannada languages. Writing is her passion. She is an active member of various literary groups on Facebook and has won several awards in poetry. Her writes are published in National and International magazines, newspapers and anthologies. Talkative by nature, she wishes to spread love and positivity through her poetry. She holds a degree of Masters of Commerce. Currently, she runs a playschool for poor kids.

24. Pleasure of Majestic Love

My pleasure for majestic love,
Makes me so good for now,
Since I want to be refreshed,
My past love kills me forever.

But I will stay so good,
I wish my world to be happy,
A place to make some deep love,
I will be the fragrance of love.

Only for you to be blessed,
And to be so happy forever,
I wish my world to be like yours,
Simplify good and also normal.

I wish my world to be full of gossip,
The fragrance of my love is true,
Since I have the power,
To make you happy and proud.

© Maid Corbic

Maid Corbic (Bosnia and Herzegovina)

detrix233@gmail.com

He is a young writer who is passionate about poetry. He also selflessly helps others around him. He is the moderator of the World Literature Forum 'World Literature Forum Peace and Humanity' in Bhutan. He is also the editor of the First Virtual Art portalled by Dijana Uherek Stevanovic and the selector of the competition on a page of the same name that aims to bring together all poets around the world his face. He is a diploma holder in graphics and web design.

25. Valentine's wish

I am an unromantic environmental officer,
But luckily having a romantic life partner.
I wanted to make his Valentine's Day beautiful,
Took the help of my friends during school.

Wrote a romantic poem,
Oh my dear husband, you are my environment.
Without you I am life without water,
Proper love and care can check the pollution forever.

Release of unnecessary words and actions,
May cause damage to our life notions.
By taking adequate measures,
We can make life a great treasure.

After reading my letter he blasts into laughter,
Said I can understand your love, my dear.
I became ashamed and said,
You are always my Valentine my dear husband.

© Manaswinee Dash Panigrahi

Manaswinee Dash Panigrahi

(Bhubaneswar, Odisha, India)
gouriraj69@gmail.com

She is a poet by passion. She is an active member of various literary groups on Facebook and has won several awards in poetry. Her writes are published in National and International magazines, newspapers and anthologies. She wishes to spread love and peace through her poetry. She is a homemaker and holds a degree of M.Sc. and M.Phil in Environmental Sciences.

26. Withered Flowers

Twinkling stars but darkness on the deck,
The galaxy smirks at my emotional wreck,
The dark night overpowered me,
A frightening silence reigns.

My bewildered self-drowned in turbulence,
Guilt-ridden, forging a smile,
Seeking my inner soul,
Overflowing with love for you.

You saw just deception,
The misapprehension about me,
My dreams encompass,
Your beautiful face.

A love blossoming like a garden,
With blooming flowers,
Now a plot of withered flowers,
Withered flowers…

© Pradnya Surve

Pradnya Surve (Mumbai, Maharashtra, India)

pradnya1260@gmail.com

She is a poet and writer. She is an active member of various literary groups on Facebook and has won several awards in poetry. Her writes are published in National and International magazines, newspapers and anthologies. She wishes to spread love and peace through her poetry. She is a homemaker and holds a degree of Postgraduate in Child Development and Family Relations.

27. Valentine's Day Valids Decency

Lovely Valentine's day is not the day
of kissing, sending rose but the day of love.
Love is angelic and seraphic
Moving in heavenly atmospheric.

Love is a gift of Almighty filled with beauty
Gift is nowhere to be found but in noble heart.
Love lengthens the span of life
filling liberty and giving lesson of affection of love.

Lessons about virtue, vice is to be lessened
in which legacy is peace, humanity and loyalty.
Love lives in empathy and sympathy 'house to live long.
Love longs last the love bond lasting long.

© Prasanna Bhatta

Prasanna Kumar Bhatta (Berhampur, Odisha, India)

prasanabhatta1@gmail.com

He is a budding writer who began writing in 2021. He is a member of various poetry groups on Facebook and actively participates in various poetry contests. He has won several awards for his poetry. He has co-authored one poetry book 'KAVYA KUMBHA' which is recognised in Indian book of records and is well accepted by the readers.He is M.A, M. Ed and is retired as principal of GVJC College.

28. Once in a Blue Moon

Once in a blue moon, I think about you,
You were my love, my heart, my soul and everything,
Sitting near the bank of the river throwing stones,
Seeing you inside the whirling water.

Once in a blue moon, you spent so many moments with me,
Remembering those days, my body is shivering now,
I'm unable to forget those heart-throbbing moments,
Missing your embrace and mellow caress.

Once in a blue moon, I went to the park in the evening time,
Where you bloomed like a flower, blossomed like a cloud,
So many rainbows could see your twinkling eyes,
So many promises, you had made.

Alas ! with time moving on…
Everything has been shattered, every dream, every thought,
Today is Valentine's day and I am searching
Where is my valentine? Where is my Love?

© Dr Prasanna Kumar Mohapatra

Dr. Prasanna Kumar Mohapatra

(Odisha, Bhubaneshwar, India)
pkmo.kbl@gmail.com

He is a budding writer who started his poetic journey 1 year ago. He is a member of various poetry groups on Facebook and has achieved a lot of recognitions of his poetry. He is a founder of a poetry group, 'United Poets@ Heart'. He is encouraging many poets and writers through his group. He is post graduate and M.Sc in Applied Mathematics. He is retired from LnT company in Odisha and working in LIC company at present.

29. Lost in Love

In love, I am lost, in love,
Clouds of lily-like love hover,
Over me and around me,
Lightening of love –
Completely surrounds me,
Showers of love, soften me.

In rains of love, roam I,
In the storm of love, I lie,
Hail me! Dear love's realm,
Under love's reign, I live
And in the vast valley of love,
Lost I am, in love's region.

Seek me, if you really wish,
But, with love, as I am in love,
Rather I have become love,
So intensely lost I am in love.

© *Promila Punnu Bhardwaj*

Promila Punnu Bhardwaj

(Shimla, Himachal Pradesh, India)
bhardwajpamela@gmail.com.

She is a bi-lingual poet who writes in English and Hindi Languages. She has authored three English and two Hindi poetry books. She is an active member of various literary groups on Facebook and participates in several poetry contests. She has won many awards for her poetry. Her poems have been published in National and International newspapers, literary magazines and anthologies. She is M. A. in English Literature and is retired General Manager, Industries Department of H.P. Government.

30. Doorway to My Soul

The doorway to my soul is through my heart,
When I let you in…
Please stay there for a while,
Look around, and feel yourself at home.
You will see my rainbow-colored dreams,
there are clouds of hope, touching the sky.
You will find an abundance of love,
It's up to you to take as much as you can.

In the right corner, you will see a rose plant, without thorns,
This is the rose you gave me at our first meeting.
You will find a few of my loved ones there too,
Some fictional characters from my favourite books,
Some broken promises and past pains you would also come across,
Just to tell you that they exist.
if you have a cure please do so, otherwise, let them heal.
But don't scratch them.

It will be your home…
Before I let you see my soul.

© Rachana Sood

Rachana Sood (Delhi, India)

rachanasekhri77@gmail.com

She is a bilingual poet who writes in English and Hindi languages. She writes under the name of 'Meethinimboli'. She is a member of various poetry groups on social media. She has contributed her poems to several anthologies, magazines, newspapers, and online-live poetry recitation events. Her writings are mainly concerned with diverse facets of human emotions and vibrant natural phenomena. She is B. A (Honours) in Tourism Studies. Currently, she is working as a Yoga owner and assisting her father in his construction company.

31. Our Grey Destiny

The moment you kissed me, I became your lips,
The moment you hugged me, I became your heart,
The moment you told me I am loved,
I became spring in your words, A purple depth in you.

The days had their feet to carry us swifter than ever,
To the land of stars and moon,
We were so bright the lamps could never know,
The dreams were so transparent.

The diamonds could ever become,
In those nights of indomitable love,
But the roads broke into zigzags,
Our hearts beat like the tail of a fish.

In sad evenings we felt like turtles lost in sand,
A grey destiny waited for us to lie alone in our rooms,
We lost our paths like travellers in deserts for an oasis,
Alas! I could not become like you In art and wisdom of love.

© Rajendra K. Padhi

Rajendra K Padhi (Bhubaneswar, Odisha, India)

rajendrapadhi62@gmail.com

He is a poet, novelist, editor and translator. He has translated many stories, biographies and poems from Odia into English. He has written 5 books including poetry and novels. His articles, poems and interviews are published in more than 80 books, and journals from different countries of the world. He has been a keynote speaker address in both National and International conferences. He is retired as a Professor in English.

32. Honey, the Love of My Life

I fell in love with her smiling face,
I fell in love seeing her doping eyes,
Her cute smile makes mine,
Her simple touch feels divine.

She changed my lifestyle,
With her love adorable,
She does bring chills to my eye,
Hence, I love her to the blue sky.

She has become my addiction,
Which seem to have no solution,
She is a God's gift and a big prize,
I always love her in king-size.

She has her own special way,
To pleasure, I love to say,
When she yells hello my boy,
The very second becomes a joy.

© Rajesh Sharma Brahmabhatla

Rajesh Sharma Brahmabhatla

(Khammam, Telangana, India)

rajeshpa09@gmail.com

He is a bilingual poet. He writes in English and Telugu languages. He is an Admin of various poetry groups on Facebook. He has authored one English poetry book entitled 'Hey Honey'. His writings are part of several anthologies, newspapers and magazines. He has received many awards for his poetry. He is BSc in Computer Science and presently works for the Government of his state in the Panchaytraj Dept.

33. Love Beyond Measures

Beyond the blaze of the sun,
All streaks of moonlight,
Peeking sneaking pearls inside the shell,
Giving luster to our companionship too,
That's nothing but my love for you.

Beneath the waves among all the seas,
By the boat of my passion,
Through infinite trust,
By the finest emotion,
I will bring my love for you,
Love beyond common sense.

Across the oceans of love,
Above all the beats of the heart,
We will fly high like wizards,
I would collect the love crystals from the peaks,
Will gift you a love blizzard.

© Ranjana Kashyap

Ranjana Kashyap (Jhakri, Himachal Pradesh, India)

ranj77in23@gmail.com

She is a poet, writer and artist. She is a member of various poetry groups on social media. She has contributed her poems to several anthologies, magazines, newspapers and blogs. Her paintings have been placed on various literary platforms. She is a passionate lover of nature. She holds the degree of M.A., B. Ed, ADCA and Art History. Presently, she is working as a professional painter.

34. My First Valentine

I first saw you riding a white scooter majestically,
Like a queen on a war horse going into a battle.

Then one day I found you in my class,
As my class fellow very keen and attentive,
I found myself seated next to you,
Like a young sibling seeking guidance,
I would pester you with my doubts,
You would answer my every query,
Very patiently like an elder sister.

Your positive vibes and motivation,
Helped me clear my tests and levels,
That period was Spring time in my life.

You went ahead for greener pastures,
In the pursuit of your career and living,
But whenever You visit me in my memories,
It's Valentine's day for me, as you were my first Valentine.

© Ravi Thakur

Ravi Thakur (Hyderabad Telangana, India)

thakur.ravims@gmail.com

He is a a multi-lingual Poet who writes in languages--English, Hindi and Telugu languages. He has published an English Poetry Anthology titled 'Angel and Phoenix '. His poems are published in various National and International anthologies, newspapers and magazines. He is an active member of several poetry groups on Facebook. His major theme of poetry is contemporary Social issues. He is a post -graduate in Hindi Literature and Psychology. He is retired as Dist. Vocational Education Officer.

35. Dear Love

It was raining from morning till noon,
When you called up and I lost my heart,
And it happened in the month of June,
Memorabilia in this lifetime.

At times, I try to erase it from my mind,
But surrender when you flash before my eyes,
I admire your art and craft,
The manner in which you hurled the bouncer.

And broke the stumps so I caught bold out,
And till this day I still adore you.
Just after my father;
The only question did you ever care or bother?

All I know as a woman needed your shoulder,
Eagerly waited to be in your tight arms,
And at last, realize I have no reason,
To call you mine.
Without you I am fine.

© Rimni Chakravarty

Rimni Chakravarty (Siliguri, West Bengal, India)

rimnichakravarty@gmail.com

She is passionate about poetry, music, art and literature. She has got more than 50 publications, 6 book chapters, and two best paper presentation awards in quest of reaching a platform in the world of literature. She is M.A.(English), B.ED and is working as Asst. Professor and Humanities.

36. My Teddy

My teddy is yet not ready,
Maybe she is scared of her daddy,
Let me not be so tidy,
And write for her a sweet melody.

So that she can cheer,
And I can present her with a Teddy Bear,
She is very smart and tells Teddy Bear,
Does not have a heart, but my dear.

If to my teddy bear you make even a slap,
It will only dance and clap,
I think this is the best thing in today's stressful life,
If you can laugh and marry in all your sufferings and strife.

My sweet lady!
You can't find a gift better, than what I gift you today,
For a happy life to marry forever,
And to live a joyful life filled with laughter.

© Rohit Dash

Rohit Dash (Bargarah, Odisha, India)

rohitdash28@gmail.com

He is a multilingual poet and writer. He writes in Odia, English, Hindi and Sambalpuri languages. So far 24 of his books has been published. He is a member of various poetry groups on Facebook. His works are also published in many International anthologies and E-zines. He has received many awards and recognition for his poetry. He is M.A. in English and is retired as a Bank Manager.

37. Love Seasons Life

The language which world considers lingua franca,
It's founding father who says that God,
Maker of all and our Lord,
Acknowledges St. Valentines' martyr for his gospel of good word.

For Adam and Eve represents not merely the opposite sex
But of the romance , love and affection perplex,
Socially, conventionally, border line barriers of all kind it over rides
Like bond between carbon atoms give shape to a diamond.

The bond between the lovers drives the saga of the world,
I be like honey bee and you be like flowering Manna dew,
He and she without these , Heaven of Eden attains not it's glory
Like gravitational force fuels cyclic Seasons.

Love fuels seasons of man,
Where joy, beauty , blissfulness and truthfulness,
Are seen be grown,
In the season said to be life.

© Sane Shiva Shankar

Sane Shiva Shanker (Mahabubnagar, Telangana, India)

saneshivashankar@gmail.com

He is a poet and writer. He is a member of various poetry groups on social media. He has contributed many poems to several anthologies, magazines, newspapers, and blogs. He is M.A (Eng.), M Phill and B.Ed. By profession, he is a senior teacher in English.

38. Rhythm of Love

Sonorous love dipped in strawberry seasoning,
Musical crochets in a fluorescent flow,
Melodious, mellifluous tone in our voice,
Together we serenade merry, love songs.

Our bond is in sync with musical concordance,
Playing upon the keys of the instruments,
Feels so joyous,
So passionate.

You and me waltzing with the zephyr,
Inebriated moods stoke us,
Come on darling,
Let us make the moments immortal.

© Seema Sharma

Seema Sharma (Delhi, India)

seemashar0807@gmail.com

She is a poet, writer and author. She is passionate about nature and reading books. She is a peace lover and believes in providing new horizons to her life. She is an active member of several literary platforms and participates in various literary activities. Her poems are part of several magazines, anthologies, and newspapers. She is a teacher by profession with MA in English.

39. The Labyrinth of Love

The dancing flame of a flickering candle,
Struggling with darkness intense to handle.
A solitary ray of light is mightier than gloom,
Moon is about to fade when fully bloomed.

Moths fanatically revolve around the flames,
Do not hesitate to sacrifice life in love's name.
Holding tightly, an unseen rope of fearlessness,
The labyrinth of love leads to endlessness.

Gleaming candles make the moths crazy,
Faint light makes the window pane hazy.
If moths learn the lesson from the dead,
Their love story would never be sacred.

*© **Shafia Afzal***

Shafia Afzal (Islamabad, Punjab, Pakistan)

afzalshafia5@gmail.com

She is a bilingual writer and poet. She writes in English and Urdu. Reading and writing have been her passion since childhood. She's a member of several renowned literary forums on social media. Her articles have been published in various National newspapers. She is a housewife and holds a degree of B.SC, in Statistics, Mathematics, and Economics.

40. Deep Feeling

When you don't have to sign,
You become my sweet Valentine.
History is attached to Such human beings,
Who has committed themselves to human Beings?

No name, no fame,
No returns and no waits.
Love is not living Together,
Getting married and Loving each other.

It is infinite and unattached,
It is blissful and devoted forever.
It is a manifestation of the angel,
Everyone is not born with Ideal parents.

It is straight from the Heart,
Nobody hints, it is a deep feeling apart.
The message we have to carry and take forward,
To become Valentine to empower and erupt like showers.

© Shelleyandra Kapil

Shelleyandra Kapil (Chandigarh, India)

kapilirts@gmail.com

He is a poet, reviewer and writer, who writes in Hindi, Punjabi and English languages. He has published 6 books. His poems are published in various literary magazines, books, newspapers and anthologies. He has achieved several awards in his professional as well as literary fields. He is M.A in Public Administration. He has retired as Principal Chief Commercial Manager from North Central railways, Prayagraj.

41. When Two Souls Combine

I saw it tonight
The minute hand of a clock was in eight.
Your heartbeat I heard so loud,
Reverberating the past story aloud.

I remember, you once carried me to the beautiful panorama,
My nose still lingers on the everlasting aroma.
You covered me from the hard wind
With your bare hands like a whirlwind.

Yesterday's memories
Take off all the Miseries.
Anger and smile walked through me
When two souls combine.

© Shwetha A

Shwetha A (Neerchal, Kerala, India)

shwetha192000@gmail.com

She is a poet, writer and author. She loves to decorate her skills with rainbow colours. With her passion for poetry and skills for creativity, she does believe that she can make a positive impact. She is an active member of various literary groups on social media. Her poems have been published in many National and International journals, anthologies, newspapers and magazines. She has won numerous accolades and diplomas for her writings. She has recently earned the degree of BE in Computer Science. Currently, she is preparing for her interviews.

42. To My Soul

In your words
I heard melodious…
Poems for me.

In your silence
I saw a river with…
The flow of emotions.

The loneliness you
Bestowed was only…
To see the sky of love.

In the myriad forms of
Relations, I couldn't see…
An innocent flower with sincere petals like you.

The sole prayer with me is to
Have your smile…
On my face always.

© Sreedharan Parokode

Sreedharan Parokode (Kozhikode, Kerala, India)

sreeparokode@gmail.com

He is a bilingual poet and lyricist. He writes in English and Malayalam languages. He has thirty books of poems to his credit and has written songs for animation films also. His poems have been well received in different platforms and discussed. He presented his poems in various National and International platforms. He has received several awards and recognitions for his poetry. He beholds the degree of MA (Eco) M.A (Eng), M.A.(Popn Studies) M Phil and a Post Graduate Diploma in Parental Education. He is retired from Calicut University.

43. Blessed Love

The gentle breeze causes a flutter in my heart,
The warmth of the Sun touches my core,
As I ponder on the past, sitting by the shore,
I think of our love as an incredible piece of art.

A design made by God that changes our destiny,
An intricate masterpiece that keeps us close,
Faith and happiness form its very source,
Which draws from nature its infinite beauty.

I wish our love thrives beyond our lives
And grows stronger with every season,
That, which cannot be shaken by time or human,
Beyond every doubt and dilemma, it survives.

My joy at this thought knows no bounds,
I see myself in your lovely, deep-set eyes,
It is my home for which I can't set a price,
I wish to dwell there and never be found.

© Srividya Subramanian

Srividya Subramanian (Chennai, Tamil Nadu, India)

srivi1971@gmail.com

She is a poet, writer, and author. She writes poetry, stories, articles and essays. She is an active member of several literary platforms on social media. Her poems are part of several magazines, anthologies, and newspapers. Her other hobbies include cooking and listening to music. She is M.A. B. Ed. She is a teacher by profession. She has won a lot of recognition for her work.

44. I will Always Love You

I will always love you, my dear child,
I can do anything for your lovely smile,
You are the answer to my prayers,
Just like an angel, sent from the heavenly father.

You are my life, you are my sunshine,
When I hold you in my arms, I feel divine,
No matter what challenges I will face in the future,
Our bond is closest to my heart that I nurture.

You came into my life when I needed you the most,
You are like pleasant weather along the sea coast,
You melt my heart away with your gentle whispers,
Especially when you call me Mom, while your eyes glitter.

You are my valentine who has filled my heart with joy and love,
You are the serenity of my life, just like a cute dove,
You are like a morning star that brightens my day,
You are the charioteer of my destiny Odyssey.

© Dr. Suboohi Jafar

Dr. Suboohi Jafar (Varanasi, Uttarpradesh, India)

suboohijafar@gmail.com

She is a young and dynamic poet, artist and singer by heart, an oncologist by profession. A Soldier in Fight against CANCER. She has won many awards and medals in her academic career. She has received several awards in poetry contests conducted by various poetic groups on Facebook.

45. My Sweetheart

Oh, my sweetheart, don't go away,
I can't express my silence,,
Please try to note my inner sense
I am too shy to say, but I hope you stay.

In the barren land of my existence,
You are the only hope that lits my darkness,
You know, I fail to weave my verses,
But I seek to remain with you and your eternal presence.

My life is devoid of any motivation,
You are the reason for my happiness,
I desire to tread on this toughest passage,
By enlightening my life, just drag me from such oblivion.

Don't ask me anything more,
I crave to behold you, forever,
Too embarrassed to confess,
Yet, except you, I cannot breathe.

© *Sudipta Mishra*

Sudipta Mishra (Bhubaneshwar, Odisha, India)

sudiptamishra71@gmail.com

She is a multi-faceted artist and dancer excelling in various fields of art and culture. She has weaved more than a hundred books. Her book, 'The Essence of Life', is credited with Amazon bestseller, and 'The Songs of My Heart' is scaling newer heights of glory. She has garnered numerous accolades in literature, including the famous Rabindranath Tagore Memorial. She regularly pens articles in newspapers as a strong female voice. She is a research scholar, perusing a Ph.D. in English.

46. I Am a Sunflower

I stand excitedly beside the wide open window,
To welcome my eternal lover, the rising Sun;
I perceive the titillating chilly morning breeze,
Arousing in my heart and body a sweet sensation.

Soon the gloomy darkness disappears from east,
The sky is painted with vibrant shades of red and yellow;
Buoyant Apollo ascends with aplomb pouring warm light,
With pleasure, I hug the sunshine feeling mellow.

I know not the time when I fell in love,
With Sun, whose resplendent glory I desire to watch;
Be it morn, noon, or evening, I follow him,
Like a Sunflower, no mortal love can be his match.

For me, Sun is not a star nor is he a God,
Full of joy I welcome him daily in the morning;
My tryst with him has countless rendezvouses,
Happily, I bid him a transient farewell in the evening.

© **Sulekha Samantaray**

Sulekha Samantaray (Bhubaneshwar, Odisha, India)

sulekhasamantaray54@gmail.com

She is a bilingual writer with twelve published books and hundreds of articles including stories, poems, essays and translations both in English and Odia languages. She has also received many literary awards for her contribution to literature. She is M.A and M. Phil in English and retired as an Associate Professor in English.

47. Melting Moments

Tempting Tempestuous,
Under Cupid's Spell,
An ethereal domain,
The serene beauty of the shore.

The glorious look of adoration,
Cuddled in each other's arms,
Lost in the speechless world,
Intoxicated by oxytocin.

Sand witnesses the footprints,
Carefree birds twittering,
In the unique world of gaiety,
A lustful union of love.

Time not heeding with haste,
Melting lasts like a flower's,
Handholding to overcome misfortunes,
Echoes the symphony of heart.

© Sulochana Narayanan

Sulochana Narayanan (Palakkad, Kerala, India)

sulsubra@gmail.com

She is a lover of arts like paintings, music and poetry. She has recently published her first book "Imprints: An Anthology of Poems". She is a member of various poetry groups on Facebook and has won several awards. She is M.A English and has done B.Ed. She is an academician by profession for the past 11 years.

48. Keep Well

O' sweetheart...
Look, Valentine's day has come,
The whole world is having fun.

But ...My heart...
Bleeding only for you,
God bless you where you are.
I can hug you in my prayers,
But God can do all well.

Reminiscence is only own thing,
That pure and green fully,
Sad and happiness enriching mind,
Making life like a rainbow,
And you ever do fragrant my soul.

© Sumi Kapahera

Sumi Kapahera (Morigaon, Assam, India)

debend557@gmail.com

She is a poet by passion. At present, she is involved with many wonderful poetry platforms and literary organizations. She has achieved many awards including Gujarat Sahitya Academy certificates. She is an M.A. in English and BED, a teacher by profession.

49. Expectation

Now there is no reason to write only a single line
To impress you; as I used to write in my teenage.
Yet, your madness permits me to send a valentine,
To your desk, written in a completely different language.

You may select it for your new anthology; or may edit
The lines to change any objectionable word or phrase.
Or without changing the cryptic message hidden in it—
You may reverse the arrow of time to bring my teenage.

I'll never be able to send shock under your sweating feet,
As you are hesitant to surrender your silenced immensity.
I'm not sure how long you will be able to tolerate my heat,
However, I'll expect you'll be receptive to enchant me.

So, my renewed muteness is translating my inner tone—
Expecting its penetration inside you when you'll be alone.

© *Swapan Kumar Rakshit*

Swapan Kumar Rakshit (Bankura, West Bengal, India)

rakshit.swapan2015@gmail.com

He is a poet and writer. His major genera of poetry is composing sonnets. He is a member of various literary groups on Facebook and actively participates in several contests. He has received many prizes for his poetry. His writings are the part of many newspapers, magazines and anthologies. He wants to be acquainted with the universal passionate minds of the poets. He is B. Sc. (Physics) B. Ed. M. A. and is working as a Physics teacher.

50. Is It Not You?

Is it not you in my mind, day in, day out dreaming?
That smile is a miracle, my heart throbs, darling.
Nights become sleepless, cicadas disturb my thoughts deeper,
You alone, your palpitation, alive always in me, dear.

A while in my dinghy boat, now oozing water as blood,
Dark hours wait moonlight, a civet smell of you thrill.
The ferry man carries you, Murky water creates shadow,
Wave like shadows of you, When can I see you clear?

Hopeless future haunts me dear, Sans you life appears a misery,
When can you come to hug me O' buddy,
Out of jaunt is the time now, restless I try a vain search,
In vain, yet I feel you dear, Do come to smile, to hug.

The ferry man is cruel,
You disappear in the mist.
That day we meet in heaven,
Beauty lives on Valentine thrill.

© ***Unnikrishnan Atiyodi***

Unnikrishnan Atiyodi (Kannur, Kerala, India)

uatiyodi@gmail.com

He is a poet and writer with 3 collections of poems in English and also essays in English entitled 'Spectrum'. He has written three books in Malayalam and contributes regularly to e-journals. He is the winner of Sahithyamanjari Puraskaram. He is postgraduate in English and is retired as a principal of Higher Secondary school.

AN ANTHOLOGY OF POEMS
(PAPERBACK, 1ST EDITION, FEBRUARY 2023)
COMPILED & EDITED BY
DR. SONIA GUPTA